SISTER MAUS

Dedicated to all Salem Students and Teachers – past, present, and future.

SISTER MAUS

Text and illustrations copyright © 2006 by John Hutton
Published by Salem Academy and College
P.O. Box 10548, Winston-Salem, North Carolina 27101-0548
www.salemacademy.com *and* www.salem.edu
All rights reserved under International and Pan-American Copyright Conventions.
This publication may not be reproduced, stored in a retrieval system or transmitted in any form or by any means
electronic, mechanical, photocopying, recording or otherwise, without the permission in writing of the publishers.

Typeset in the United States of America by Carrie Leigh Dickey
Printed and bound in the United States of America by Keiger Printing Company, Inc.
FIRST LIMITED EDITION, first printing

ISBN 978-0-9789608-0-3
0-9789608-0-7

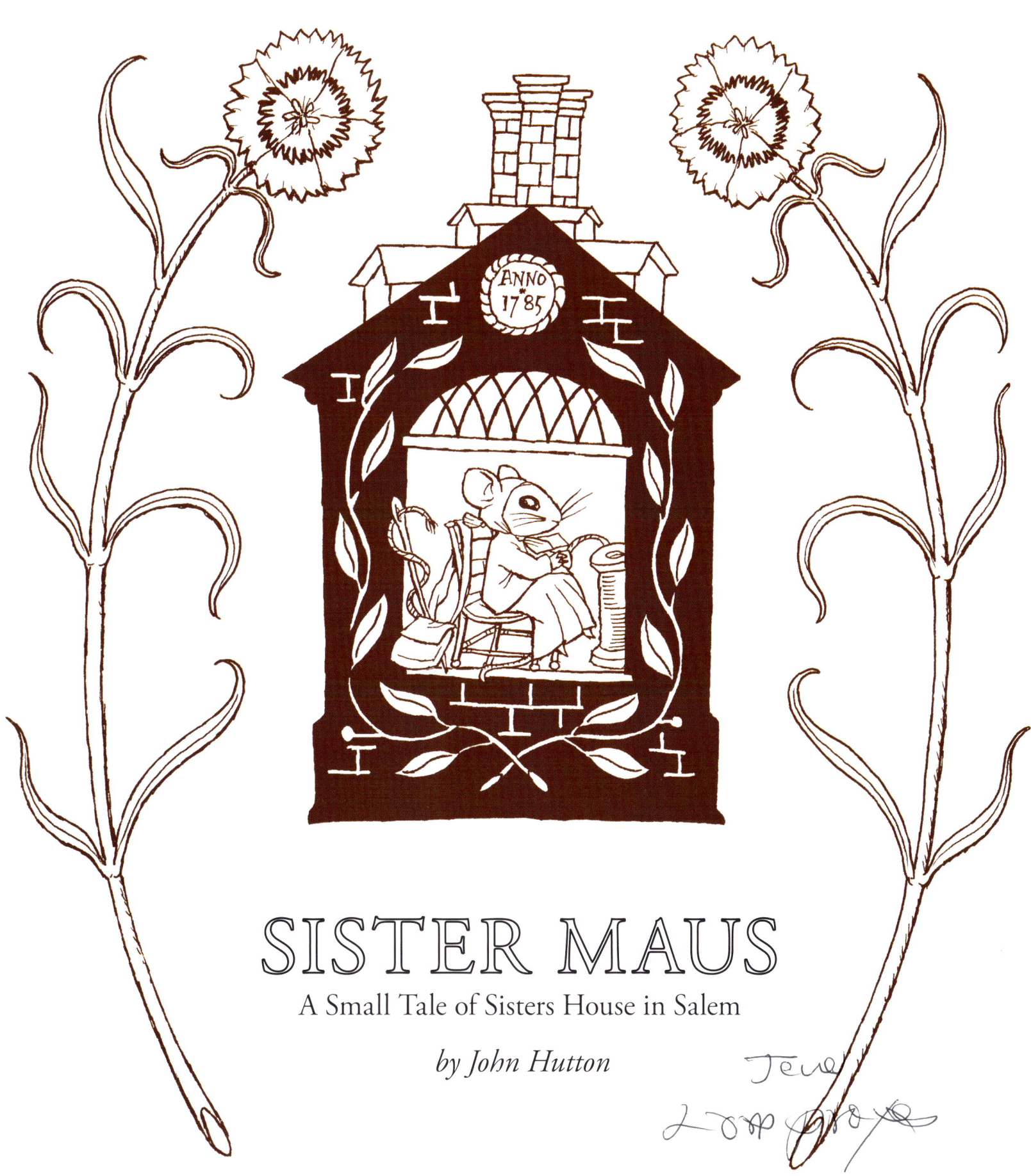

SISTER MAUS

A Small Tale of Sisters House in Salem

by John Hutton

SALEM ACADEMY AND COLLEGE
2006

Long Ago in Old America, there

lived a mouse in a town called SALEM, at the edge of the Wilderness. The mouse was named Maus Kraus, and she lived in Sisters House. Sisters House was where all the older girls and single women lived until they decided to get married. And the single Brothers – they had a Brothers House. And the Families – they each had a Family house. How *very unusual* were the customs of olden times in Salem!

In those days the LITTLE GIRLS OF SALEM could not read, and they wanted to read. They could not count, and they wanted to count. And so the Elders of the town sent word up North, to Bethlehem, Pennsylvania – they themselves had lived there once – for a *reading and counting teacher*. And Catherine, it turned out, was the one who was asked, and the one who came.

Catherine came with some Others. These were the SEVEN STRONG GIRLS, who walked down from Bethlehem to Salem together, **Five Hundred Miles!** The Seven often stopped to mend their socks as they walked the long walk. And all unknown to them, in their sewing basket, carried by Catherine – was Maus Kraus!

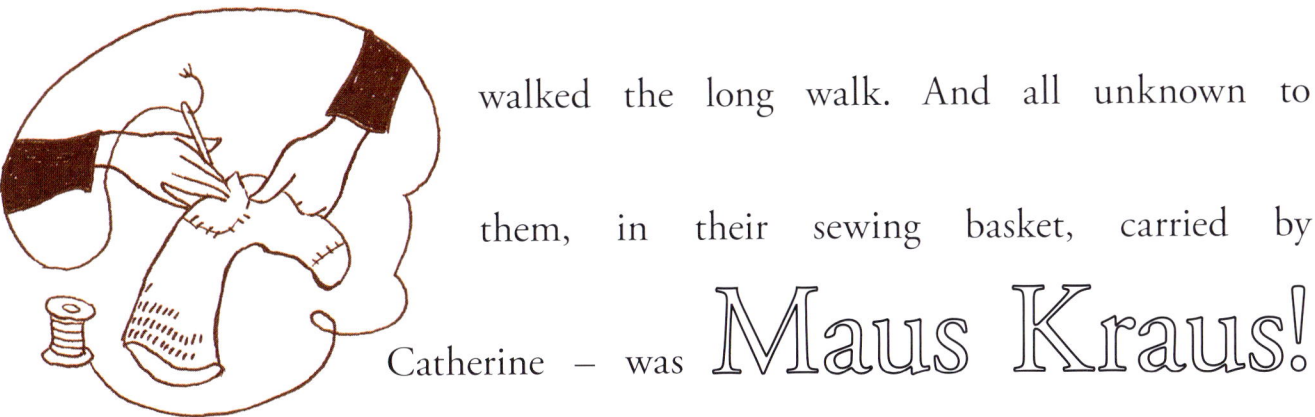

She had fallen asleep in the *comfortable* basket, filled with linen scraps, up in Bethlehem. "How very interesting!" said Maus Kraus as she watched the sewing. She soon made clothes for herself just like the girls – a long skirt, a short jacket, and a cap. "Sehr Schön! How fine you look, Maus Kraus!" she said happily. "So useful a thing, for a mouse to learn to sew!"

At last the Seven Strong Girls came to Salem, and naturally they opened the door and went to live in Sisters House. The Strong Girls left their bags and baskets in the hall. And POP! Maus Kraus followed them into the Sisters House and suddenly disappeared down a small hole in the wall.

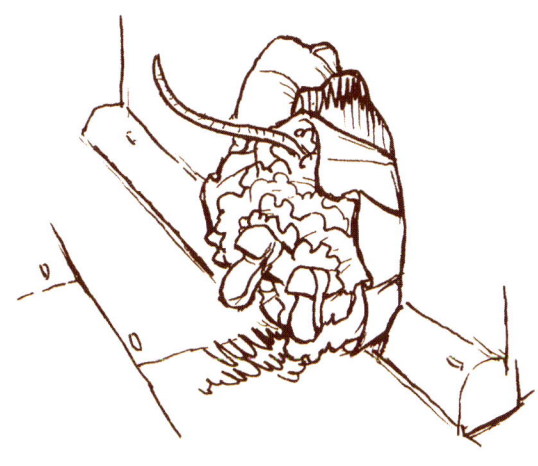

Sisters House was a very fine place for Strong Girls, but also a very fine place for mice. Maus Kraus was warmly greeted by the Head Mouse. There were *many* rooms and stairs and passages in the Maus House tucked behind the walls of Sisters House. "The Mice are all very kind!" thought Maus Kraus. "I shall be happy here!"

Maus Kraus liked to do her washing on Tuesdays, in a small tin cup which she found behind a cabinet in the kitchen. The wash house, where the Sisters did their laundry, was outside, in the garden. Oh no!
Frau Kater – Mrs Cat!

What an unpleasant surprise for Maus Kraus!

Luckily, Maus Kraus had her sewing needle. **Watch out, Frau Kater!** But it was not really Maus Kraus who frightened away Frau Kater. It was Sister Catherine. She had just come into the garden. "Was tust du, Schwesterlein? What are you doing, Little Sister?" said the girl to the mouse. She was very surprised to see a mouse wearing a skirt and a cap and a jacket — *just like a Sister!*

Sister Catherine tucked Maus Kraus into the pocket of her apron. "You will come with me to School, Sister Maus, where you will be safe. The Little Girls will love to meet you!"

Sister Catherine's School for Little Girls was in the Gemeinhaus, the town hall, next to Sisters House.

Maus Kraus curtsied very prettily for the Little Girls. "Guten Tag, guten Tag, Schwester Maus! Hello, Hello, Sister Maus!"

What an enchanting new friend! Such very nice manners!

Maus Kraus came to school every day with Sister Catherine. Sister Catherine taught the girls how to read and to write in English and in German, and how to count and sing and sew. Maus Kraus was *delighted* with the lessons. **But her favorite subject was sewing.** How straight and fine and small were her stitches!

"Sister Maus, Sister Maus, would you please help me with my embroidery!" cried the Little Girls, each one. Of course she would!

A Sampler by Sister Maus

One day after school, Sister Catherine rushed back to Sisters House. She was very excited. There were new books with  pictures in Brother Traugott's store, just across the square! Was there any extra money to buy the books? The Elders said No. Poor Little Girls! 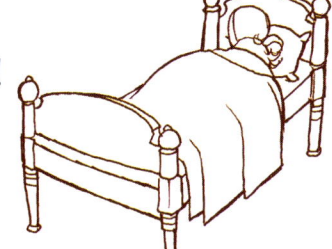 Sister Catherine went sadly to bed.

But wait! Maus Kraus had heard everything. Soon she had a wonderful idea. She ran down the passages and up the stairs behind the walls, straight to Sister Catherine's room.

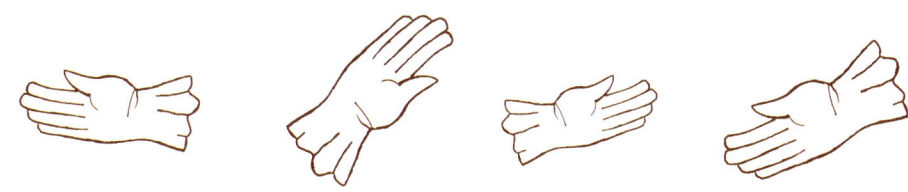

Maus Kraus knew that the Sisters sometimes made gloves to sell to Brother Traugott. She found a basket full of scraps. Snip, snap, snip!

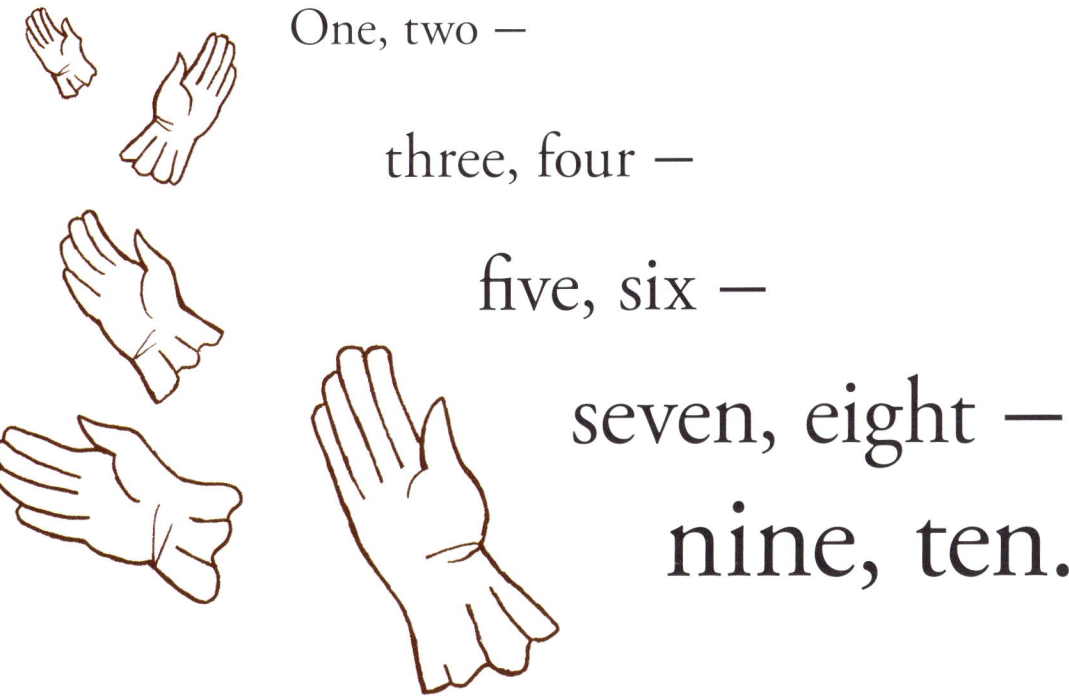

One, two —

    three, four —

        five, six —

            seven, eight —

                nine, ten.

She sewed gloves, and gloves, and more gloves!

Maus Kraus fell asleep, at last, in the sewing basket. **How surprised Sister Catherine was the next morning.** Ten fine pairs of gloves. *Who had made them?*

Why, it was Sister Maus! There she was – her furry little self, with a needle still clutched in her paw.

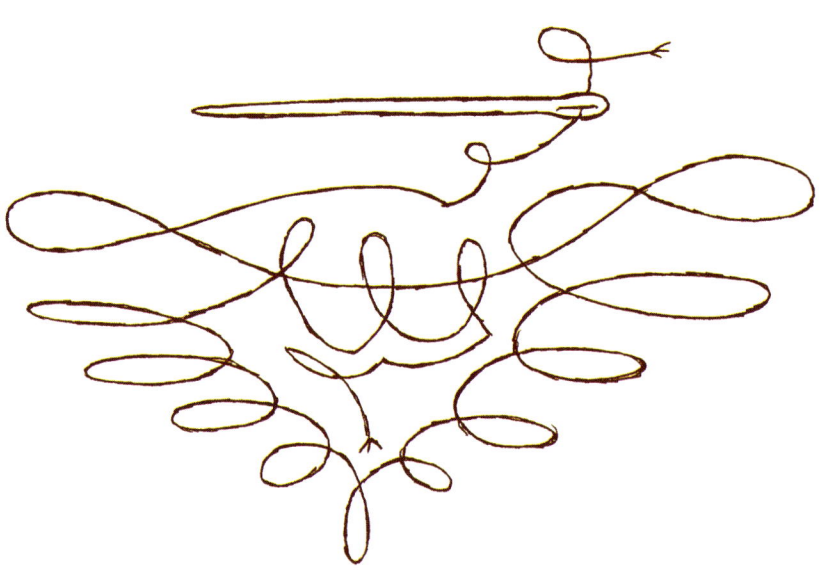

Sister Catherine ran across the square to Brother Traugott's store. He was very happy to buy the gloves – so finely made! Sister Catherine proudly came back with an *armful* of books. **Beautiful books for all the Little Girls!**

From that day on, Brother Traugott bought everything that Maus Kraus could make. Sister Catherine said that they would soon have enough money to pay for a new school building –

– and perhaps, *some day*, also a college – in the town of Salem, at the edge of the Wilderness! Thank you, Thank you, Sister Maus.

THE END

SPECIAL THANKS

Salem Academy and College gratefully acknowledges the generous support of the Sam N. Carter and Pauline Carter Fund of the Winston-Salem Foundation and grantmaking partner Charlie Hemrick for making this book possible.

Special thanks are also due to Penny Niven, Gwynne Taylor, Jane Carmichael and Johanna Brown for their encouragement in bringing this project to completion.

AUTHOR'S NOTES

This book is based on the early days of Salem Academy and College, an academic institution for women founded in 1772 in the village of Salem, in the Moravian settlement called Wachovia, in northwestern North Carolina. Sisters House actually still exists on the Salem College campus in Winston-Salem, North Carolina, and visitors are encouraged to come to see Sister Maus's historic mouse hole!

Many features of the story are derived from Salem's own history, especially the years between the completion of Sisters House in 1786 and, in 1805, the building of a new structure (now South Hall on Salem College's campus). Before 1805, Salem students were taught in a room in the Gemeinhaus, the town hall of Salem. The school was originally called The Little Girls' School.

Sister Catherine's five-hundred-mile journey on foot from "up North" is a reflection of an actual trip made by Sister Elizabeth Oesterlein and fifteen female companions in 1766. They traveled from the Moravian settlement at Bethlehem, Pennsylvania, to Bethabara in the Moravian settlement in North Carolina. Most of the settlers of Bethabara later moved to Salem in 1772. Sister Oesterlein was the first teacher (1772-1780) of the Little Girls' School in Salem.

The fictional Sister Catherine's name is borrowed from the historical Sister Catherine Sehner, who was Salem's second teacher (1780-1791). She was the first Salem teacher to actually live in Sisters House.

Because most of the Moravians were of German extraction, German was the language of official, church and home life in Salem until the middle of the nineteenth century. Therefore, I have included simple German phrases, with English translations, at several points in the story.

In the eighteenth and nineteenth centuries, most aspects of life in Salem were guided by a person's "choir." Choirs were social groups organized by age, gender and marital status. For instance, as members of the Single Sisters Choir, young unmarried women and older single women lived together in Sisters House.

Because the Sisters worked hard to support themselves and contribute to the economy of the Salem community, Sisters House was surrounded by outbuildings, gardens and animal pens. The wash house to which Sister Maus was traveling when she met Frau Kater was one of those outbuildings. It is currently in use as the Alumnae House at Salem College.

The beautiful picture books desired by Sister Catherine in the story are, in fact, a Moravian invention. Bishop John Amos Comenius (1592-1670), an important Moravian leader and educator, is credited with creating the first illustrated book for teaching children, the *Orbis Sensualium Pictus* of 1658. Bishop Comenius' ideas also influenced the Moravians' strong belief that girls should be educated as well as boys.

The curriculum of the Little Girls' School included reading and writing in English and German. Other subjects taught included arithmetic, singing and sewing. Many works of embroidery made by students in the school have been preserved in the collections of Salem Academy and College, the Old Salem museum buildings, and the Museum of Early Southern Decorative Arts, Old Salem, Inc. Many of the other objects illustrated in this book, such as furniture, fire buckets, and sewing implements, were also drawn from actual historic objects in these collections.

The Single Sisters, including teachers in the Little Girls' School, were known to have made gloves to earn extra money in the eighteenth and nineteenth centuries.

From 1772-1800, Traugott Bagge, called Brother Traugott in the story, ran the Salem Community Store across Salem Square from Sisters House.

The Little Girls' School became known to the Salem community as the Girls' Boarding School in 1805 when the new school building was finished. According to early advertisements, variations on this name were also used, such as the Girls' Boarding School for Female Education. By the 1850's, the school had come to be known as Salem Female Academy. In 1907 the official name was changed to the current form: Salem Academy and College. The academic programs of the academy and the college separated in 1912, and the academy moved to its own nearby campus in 1930. I am indebted to the late Susan O. Taylor, reference librarian at Salem College, for clarifying this information.

Finally, it is an open question as to whether the sale of mouse-stitched gloves made any of this expansion possible. Documents in the Moravian Archives neither confirm nor deny this theory!

John Hutton has taught in the Art Department at Salem College since 1990. He lives in Winston-Salem, and was educated at Princeton and Harvard. He is the author and illustrator of *The White House ABC: A Presidential Alphabet* (2004), and *Alphababel, an Illustrated Tower of Languabets* (2001).